You've got a friend, Charlie Brown

Charles M. Schulz

Selected Cartoons from
YOU'LL FLIP, CHARLIE BROWN, Vol. I

CORONET BOOKS
Hodder Fawcett, London

Copyright © 1965, 1966, 1967 by
United Feature Syndicate, Inc.

First published by Fawcett Publications Inc.,
New York 1972

Coronet edition 1973
Eighth impression 1978

———————————————

Printed in Great Britain for Hodder
Fawcett Ltd., Mill Road, Dunton Green,
Sevenoaks, Kent (Editorial Office:
47 Bedford Square, London, WC1 3DP) by
C. Nicholls & Company Ltd
The Philips Park Press, Manchester

ISBN 0 340 17417 X

ARE YOU GOING TO BE A NEWSPAPER BOY WHEN YOU GET OLDER, CHARLIE BROWN?

WELL, I'D LIKE TO BE... YES, I THINK I'D LIKE TO HAVE MY OWN ROUTE..

THEN YOU SHOULD LEARN HOW TO ROLL AND FOLD A PAPER SO YOU CAN TOSS IT ONTO A DOOR STEP...HERE, LET ME SHOW YOU...

ONLY TWO MORE DAYS UNTIL BEETHOVEN'S BIRTHDAY!
THIS ANNOUNCEMENT VOID WHERE PROHIBITED BY LAW
SCHULZ

© 1970 United Feature Syndicate, Inc.

Wherever Paperbacks Are Sold

THE WONDERFUL WORLD OF PEANUTS

☐	12544 6	What Next, Charlie Brown (26)	60p
☐	15135 8	You're the Greatest, Charlie Brown (27)	60p
☐	15829 8	It's For You Snoopy (28)	50p
☐	15828 X	Have It Your Way, Charlie Brown (29)	50p
☐	15698 8	You're Not For Real Snoopy (30)	50p
☐	15696 1	You're a Pal, Snoopy (31)	60p
☐	16712 2	What Now Charlie Brown (32)	50p
☐	17322 X	You're Something Special Snoopy (33)	50p
☐	17417 X	You've Got A Friend, Charlie Brown (34)	50p
☐	17844 2	Take It Easy, Charlie Brown (35)	50p
☐	17861 2	Who Was That Dog I Saw You With, Charlie Brown? (36)	50p
☐	18303 9	There's No-one like you Snoopy (37)	60p
☐	18663 1	Your Choice Snoopy (38)	50p
☐	18831 6	Try It Again Charlie Brown (39)	50p
☐	19550 9	You've Got It Made Snoopy (40)	50p
☐	19858 3	Don't Give Up Charlie Brown (41)	50p
☐	19927 X	You're So Smart Snoopy (42)	60p
☐	20491 5	You're On Your Own Snoopy (43)	60p
☐	20754 X	You Can't Win Them All Charlie Brown (44)	50p
☐	21236 5	It's All Yours Snoopy (45)	50p
☐	21797 9	Watch Out Charlie Brown (46)	50p
☐	21983 1	You've Got To Be You, Snoopy (47)	50p
☐	22159 3	You've Come a Long Way, Snoopy (48)	60p
☐	22304 9	That's Life Snoopy (49)	50p
☐	22778 8	It's Your Turn Snoopy (50)	50p

Numbers 1-25 and all the above Peanuts titles are available at your local bookshop or newsagent, or can be ordered direct from the publisher. Just tick the titles you want and fill in the form below.
Prices and availability subject to change without notice.

CORONET BOOKS, P.O. Box 11, Falmouth, Cornwall.
Please send cheque or postal order, and allow the following for postage and packing:
U.K.—One book 22p plus 10p per copy for each additional book ordered, up to a maximum of 82p.
B.F.P.O. and EIRE—22p for the first book plus 10p per copy for the next 6 books, thereafter 4p per book.

OTHER OVERSEAS CUSTOMERS—30p for the first book and 10p per copy for each additional book.

Name ....

Address ....

....